This edition published by Parragon Books Ltd in 2015 and distributed by

Parragon Inc.
440 Park Avenue South, 13th Floor
New York, NY 10016
www.parragon.com

ISBN 978-1-4723-4977-4

Printed in China

DISNEY · PIXAR

THE GOOD DINOSAUR

All About Me!

PaRRagon

Bath · New York · Cologne · Melbourne · Delhi
Hong Kong · Shenzhen · Singapore · Amsterdam

This book belongs to

....

....

All About You!

Arlo is the youngest member of a family of Apatosauruses.
He loves his life on the farm, where his Poppa and Momma
work hard to look after their three children.

Let's Learn about you!

Name: ....

Birthday: ....

Hair color: ....

Height: ....

Stick a photo of
yourself here!

Baby-saurus

When Arlo was born, he was very small and unsteady on his feet. What were you like when you were a baby? Add some cute baby pictures of yourself on these pages.

Meet the Family!

Arlo belongs to a loving family. His Poppa is devoted to the farm and family, and his Momma looks after everyone. Arlo also has a sister called Libby, and a brother called Buck.

HENRY–Poppa

IDA–Momma

ARLO–Little Brother

LIBBY–Big Sister

BUCK–Big Brother

Now draw your own family below.
Don't forget to write down who's who!

A Day Out

Poppa takes Arlo into a field on the farm to show him the fireflies. At first, Arlo is scared of the insects—but then Poppa shows him how to make the bugs glow! Write about a fun family outing that you enjoyed.

One day, my family went to... ....

....

....

....

....

....

....

....

....

Sometimes it's a good idea to write down your thoughts about your family. You might discover things that you never knew!

Who makes me laugh the most? ....
....
....

Who spends the most time with me? ....
....
....

Who am I most like? ....
....

Who gives the best hugs? ....
....

Me and My Friend

Arlo's best friend is Spot—but who is yours? Draw a picture of your friend in the space below. Then write down your three favorite things about them on the opposite page.

MY BEST FRIEND

.... **is my best friend because...**

1. ....

....

☐

2. ....

....

☐

3. ....

....

☐

Can you pick your top favorite thing about your friend?
Check the box next to one you think is most important.

Friendly Faces

Use these pages to add pictures of all of your best buds!

Conquer Your Fear!

Arlo is scared of what's beyond his family's farm. Everyone is afraid of something—it's perfectly normal! One way of getting over your fears is to face them, so try drawing something that scares you.

Pet Collector

Arlo meets many strange characters on his adventure through the wilderness. One of them, called Forrest Woodbush, collects different kinds of animals. Write about your own pets here.

Name: ....

Nickname: ....

Type of animal: ....

Favorite food: ....

Best thing about them: ....

....

....

If you don't have any pets, make some up! Let your imagination run wild!

Name: ....

Nickname: ....

Type of animal: ....

Favorite food: ....

Best thing about them: ....

....

....

Name: ....

Nickname: ....

Type of animal: ....

Favorite food: ....

Best thing about them: ....

....

....

Foraging for Food

Spot knows all about finding food in the wild. He'll eat anything from berries to bugs. What kind of food do you like to eat? Write down your favorite meals and snacks—and draw a picture of them, too!

MEAT!

Favorite kind: ....

....

Best served with: ....

....

Breakfast, lunch, or dinner? ....

I like it because: ....

....

VEGETABLES!

Favorite kind: ....

....

Best served with: ....

....

Breakfast, lunch, or dinner? ....

I like it because: ....

....

FRUIT!

Favorite kind: ....

....

Best served with: ....

....

Breakfast, lunch, or dinner? ....

I like it because: ....

....

Into the Wild!

Arlo was scared of the wilderness beyond his farm, but then he went on an incredible journey. It taught him there are all kinds of places in the world. If you could go on a wild adventure, where would you go? Draw a map of your imaginary trip!

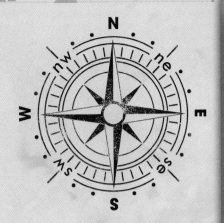

Places you could include:

Mountains, rivers, marshlands, volcanoes, forests, plains, farms, towns, oceans, caves, and anything else you can think of!

Dinosaurs Rule!

How much do you love dinosaurs? Check the footprint next to your favorite dinosaur.

Apatosaurus

Tyrannosaurus

Velociraptor

Styracosaurus

Dino Decider

Arlo is an Apatosaurus. What kind of dinosaur or prehistoric reptile would you be? Take the test and find out, then draw the result on the opposite page!

I am...

1. Kind   2. Tough   3. Mean

I get around on...

1. All fours   2. Two legs   3. Wings

If I see a helpless creature, I will...

1. Help it   2. Ignore it   3. Eat it

I mostly eat...

1. Berries   2. Crocodiles   3. Anything

My favorite thing in the world is...

1. Family ☐   2. Fighting ☐   3. Storms ☐

How Did You Do?

Mostly 1s

You're an Apatosaurus!

Mostly 2s

You're a T. rex!

Mostly 3s

You're a Pterodactyl!

Draw your dino here!

Dino Dream Diary

Arlo dreams of making his mark one day. Use this diary to record your dreams for a week. Keep this book by your bed so you can write in it as soon as you wake up—otherwise you might forget what you dreamed about!

Monday Night ....

_____

_____

Tuesday Night ....

_____

_____

Wednesday Night ....

_____

_____

Thursday Night _____

_____

_____

Friday Night _____

_____

_____

Saturday Night _____

_____

_____

Sunday Night _____

_____

_____

Family Album

Family is very important to Arlo. When he gets lost in the wilderness he has to close his eyes to picture the faces of his loved ones. Stick photographs of your family members in this album.

Home Sweet Home

When Arlo gets lost in the wilderness, he thinks of home. Would you miss your home? Write about it below and draw a picture of your house on the next page.

Location: ....

House ☐   Apartment ☐   Trailer ☐

Number of rooms: ....

Favorite room: ....

Favorite neighbor: ....

....

....

Draw your home here!

Your Heroes

Arlo looks up to his Poppa as a hero. Who are your heroes?
Write about your real-life sports, school, family, and movie
heroes here.

My Sports Hero

Name: ....

My hero because: ....

....

....

What I like best about them: ....

....

....

....

My School Hero

Name: ....

My hero because: ....

....

....

What I like best about them: ....

....

....

....

My Family Hero

Name: ....

My hero because: ....

....

....

What I like best about them: ....

....

....

....

My Movie Hero

Name: ....

My hero because: ....

....

....

What I like best about them: ....

....

....

....

Keeping Track

Spot can track a herd of longhorns across miles of open wilderness. But how good are you at keeping track of birthdays? Use this book to make sure you never miss a single one!

Name: ....

Birthday: ....

Age: ....

Ideas for presents: ....

Friend ☐   Family ☐   Pet ☐

Name: ....

Birthday: ....

Age: ....

Ideas for presents: ....

Friend ☐   Family ☐   Pet ☐

Name: ....

Birthday: ....

Age: ....

Ideas for presents: ....

Friend ☐   Family ☐   Pet ☐

Name: ....

Birthday: ....

Age: ....

Ideas for presents: ....

Friend ☐   Family ☐   Pet ☐

Name: ....

Birthday: ....

Age: ....

Ideas for presents: ....

Friend ☐   Family ☐   Pet ☐

Name: ....

Birthday: ....

Age: ....

Ideas for presents: ....

Friend ☐   Family ☐   Pet ☐

Name: ....

Birthday: ....

Age: ....

Ideas for presents: ....

Friend ☐   Family ☐   Pet ☐

Name: ....

Birthday: ....

Age: ....

Ideas for presents: ....

Friend ☐   Family ☐   Pet ☐

Brave and Bold

After feeling afraid all the time, Arlo realizes that he is brave when he stands up to some Raptors. Write about a time that you felt brave, and draw a picture of yourself on the opposite page.

Where were you?..

....

....

What did you do?..

....

....

....

Who was there?..

....

....

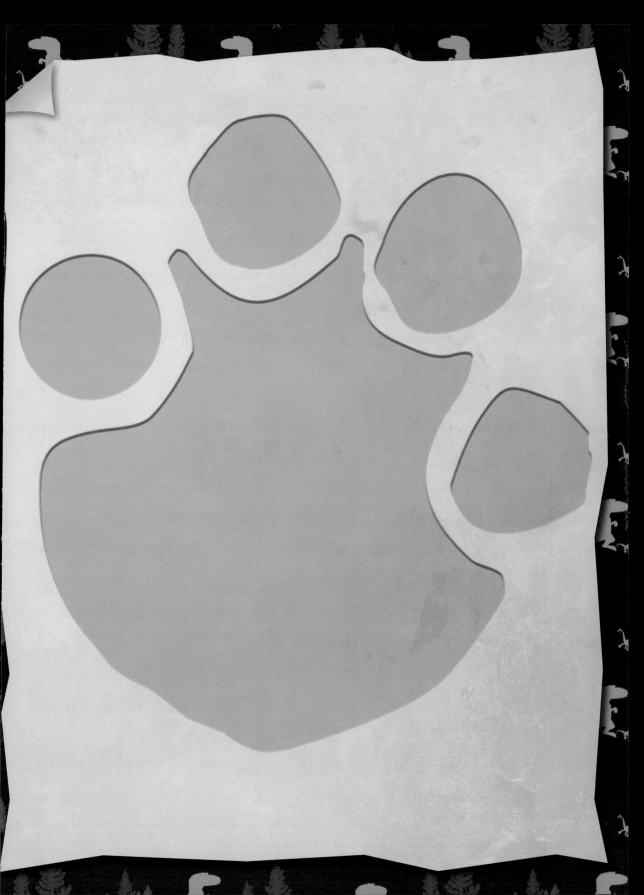